Black Girl

ENTREPRENEUR

Inspirational Journal To Write In

This Journal Belongs to:

_____

In loving memory of
Tonja Monique Wilson-Drew

Black Self-Care *Journal Series is a debut of inspirational journals written by Author Stephanie Tennille. The daily affirmations and self-love quotes offered in these journals are inspirational for self-healing, empowerment, and to help every individual to the highest version of self. These journals are for the times when self-doubt starts rearing its ugly head, and you feel weak and ready to give up. Or for when you need a reminder to love yourself and that your dreams matter, open one of these journals.*

Black Girl Entrepreneur *is the first journal in this series. You will find a mixture of motivational quotes and positive affirmations to help you reach the goals that you set for yourself. Use the writing prompts to help record your thoughts, breakthroughs, and revelations.*

Allow this journal to help you stay on track and give you the motivation you need to keep striving for success.

Remember, you are worthy.

Hold your head up queen.

I have not failed; I am simply mid-conquer.

I will keep going.

In dark times, I still shine.

I can be exhausted, but I will never be defeated.

I am on the path to great success.
I will sprinkle black girl magic
every step of the way.

I am black, beautiful, and necessary.
No one can tell me different today
or any other day.

When you're at a point of growing out of your comfort zone, it is so essential to have people that support and lift you up.

I am worthy of my success and claiming it.

Keep watering yourself. You are growing, and the next version of you is powerful.

I will stop stressing about what I can't do, and just do what I can today.

Be mindful how you talk to yourself. Make sure when you speak to yourself, they are words filled with motivation, encouragement, and love. It's essential to your growth.

I am Resilient. I will hold my head high on the worst days imaginable, so that they can become the best days possible.

Keep focusing on whatever is important to you.
Your family. Your goals. Your business.
Just stay focused.

You are the bag. Secure yourself.

If you think people are going to always be there for, you're pretty much setting yourself up for disaster. Learn to handle your own.

My peace of mind is worth more than whatever is stressing me out. I will make peace with it and move on.

Do you. What others are doing is none of your business. Focus on what you are doing.

Dear Self: I know that you don't have everything figured out. I just appreciate that you want to keep learning and growing to become the best version of self.

The enemy will try anything in its power to stop you from reaching your full potential. But always remember, the enemy has been defeated.

Keep going.

Woman of God first, businesswomen second.

It's okay for to cry. Tears help cleanse the soul and water new life at the same time.

Work on learning to accept the things that you cannot change. For the sake of your mind, it is necessary.

It's amazing how when you speak things you want into existence, and continue to work towards them; they'll come to you. Claim it.

Time doesn't stop for anyone, so what are you waiting for? Just do it.

Associate yourself with like-minded individuals. If you seek a successful life, surround yourself with the correct support system.

Realization is everything. Growth is continuous.

If your aspirations aren't frightening,

you're not living.

Life is only as good as your mindset.

Not everyone will understand what you're doing,
and why you're doing it, or where you're
going. And that's okay.
Just focus on getting there.

Your level up is going to require

more of you, stay consistent.

Currently, I'm only accepting good vibes and money.

Everyone that calls your name is not worthy of your answer. Reclaim your time and stay focused on your goals.

I am deserving of a circle that lifts and encourages me. My circle will motivate and inspire me. Quality over quantity always.

I am going to get this business off the ground by any means necessary.

Actually, I can have a seat at the table.

I am not willing to settle in any aspect of my life.

It's never to late to switch things up for the better. You owe no explanations. Go, do, and be.

I am so in love with the woman, I'm transforming into daily.

Thank you God for continuing to give me the strength to press forward on my journey and not give up.

If it's not a challenge, it won't be a change.

My motivation has to match my dreams.

Don't announce it. Just do it.

Planting the seeds is necessary to reap

the harvest I want.

Write your goals and follow through

with an action plan.

God, I let go. Do your thing.

Build yourself, and then build everything

else around you.

Difficult roads often lead to beautiful

destinations. Trust the process.

Nothing can stop a woman who walks with God, and have a plan.

Speed doesn't matter. Forward is forward.

Keep moving. Don't expect much

if there's no effort.

You are not being blocked, you are being reassigned. Keep aiming higher.

God has a plan, and my victory will be glorious.

Collect your wins with gratitude.

Stop letting who you were, talk you out of who you're becoming.

Be a lover of positivity, dope vibes,
and minding the business that pays you.

Don't be afraid to sit in the front
row of your life.

Shout out to all the women that can water themselves and still pour into others; this is for you. I love you.

Stephanie Tennille

www.ingramcontent.com/pod-product-compliance
Lightning Source LLC
Chambersburg PA
CBHW071209220526
45468CB00002B/552